Love is My Religion:

The Art of Loving Completely – Mind, Body, and Spirit

Kevin J. Houston

Published by

K & K Houston Publishing
(a division of K & K Houston Services, LLC)

ISBN: 978-0-9796524-9-3

Printed in the USA

Table of Contents

- **Love as a Path to Connection**
  - Exploring Love in Diverse Spiritual Traditions
  - Recognizing the Spiritual Energy of Love
- **Practices of Sacred Love**
  - Loving-Kindness Meditation, Prayer, Gratitude
- **Personal Stories**: Journeys of Spiritual Awakening Through Love
- **Reflection**: Deepening Your Spiritual Practice Through Love

Chapter 4: The Physical Dimension of Love

- **Love in Motion**
  - Expressing Love Through Action and Habits
  - Physical Expressions: Touch, Kindness, Acts of Service
- **Exercise**: Daily Practices to Embody Love
- **Reflection**: Extending Love to The Planet and Community
  - Environmental Responsibility and Social Engagement

Chapter 5: Navigating Love in the Modern World

- **Loving in the Age of Disconnection**

- The Impact of Technology and Social Media on Love
- Building Meaningful Connections in a Digital Age
- **Radical Compassion**
  - Love as a Response to Conflict and Division
  - Practicing Forgiveness and Empathy
- **Reflection**: Choosing Compassion Over Division

Chapter 6: The Healing Power of Love

- **Healing Through Love**
  - Love's Role in Emotional and Mental Health
  - Overcoming Trauma, Anxiety, and Depression
- **Exercise**: Strengthening Your "Love Muscles"
  - Practical Challenges to Grow Your Capacity for Love

Chapter 7: Love as a Collective Force

- **Global Love: Creating a Ripple Effect**
  - How Individual Acts of Love Inspire Societal Change
  - Movements and Stories of Collective Love in Action
- **Reflection**: Love as Social Activism

About the author

Kevin J. Houston is the author of *25 Success Principles: For Creating a Totally New You*, an IT consultant, a life and success coach, and a motivational speaker.

Born and raised in Birmingham, Alabama, Kevin is the youngest of two brothers and one sister. Growing up, he was a child who always strived for greatness. Kevin was a natural leader who consistently helped his peers achieve more. He began writing and creating positive and motivational content as early as age ten, crafting encouraging poems and songs that uplifted others. At the age of thirteen, he wrote and directed his first inspirational play as an assignment for his middle school English class.

Kevin has worked in the information technology support field for over twenty years, assisting end users and clients with resolving technical computer and system security issues. This work has enabled him to learn extensively about people, their lives, and how these factors affect them daily. The individuals he encountered in his day-to-day work and conversations were at various stages in their lives and careers.

Kevin quickly developed patience and active-listening skills. People frequently sought and still seek his opinions or advice regarding situations they faced at work with coworkers or at home with family or friends.

Kevin has spoken with a diverse range of individuals about their lives and careers, including students, facility workers, managers, directors, doctors, lawyers, entertainers, and high-level executives. These individuals share a commonality: they face real problems, regardless of their circumstances.

Another lesson Kevin learned is that people often want and need to talk to someone at these times; however, they prefer to confide in someone they trust, who can provide valuable feedback and sound advice. He attributes these varied life experiences to his desire to write, motivate, and encourage others.

Kevin has encountered many experiences throughout his life, which he feels compelled to share with others through his speaking and writing. He believes the wisdom and knowledge he has gained can benefit others. His life goal is to motivate and encourage everyone he meets.

Introduction

"Love is My Religion: The Art of Loving Completely — Mind, Body, and Spirit"

We often describe love as simply an emotion—fleeting, conditional, and confined to romantic relationships. Yet, what if love is far more profound, more enduring, and indeed, more transformative? What if love is not just an emotion but a comprehensive way of life, a guiding principle that can reshape how we think, feel, and act?

In this book, we journey beyond conventional views of love to explore it as a holistic belief system that transcends traditional boundaries. Love becomes the cornerstone of mental clarity, spiritual depth, and physical well-being. It is a commitment to live fully, compassionately, and purposefully, influencing every facet of our lives.

Understanding Love as a Holistic Life Practice

Understanding love holistically involves recognizing it not merely as a transient feeling but as a deliberate practice encompassing mental, spiritual, and physical dimensions. Holistic love is mindful and intentional, extending compassion and empathy beyond familiar circles to include all humanity, the environment, and oneself. It includes cultivating loving thoughts, nurturing spiritual connections, and embodying love through everyday actions and interactions.

To practice love holistically is to engage actively with life through consistency and intentional mindfulness. This approach requires self-awareness and the ongoing alignment of our thoughts, beliefs, and behaviors with the principles of compassion, empathy, and interconnectedness. Holistic love inspires us to cultivate deeper relationships, promote healing, and make positive contributions to our communities and the environment.

Why This Matters: Love Beyond Conventional Boundaries

Why should we extend our understanding of love beyond conventional boundaries? Our traditional notions of love, limited to emotional bonds or romantic attachments, often overlook its broader potential to heal and unify. In an increasingly fragmented and polarized world, embracing love as a holistic practice is not merely beneficial—it is essential.

Love that transcends conventional boundaries has the power to dissolve barriers of misunderstanding and prejudice, fostering genuine empathy and connectedness among diverse groups. It encourages emotional resilience, promotes mental well-being, and cultivates spiritual growth.

Ultimately, practicing holistic love enriches our lives, strengthens our communities, and helps build a more compassionate and inclusive world.

Consider this your invitation to redefine love in your life—to see it not merely as something you feel but as something you actively choose and live by daily. By choosing love as your religion, you declare that love is not just part of life but the essence of a meaningful and fulfilling existence.

Let us begin this journey together, guided by love as our guiding principle, our religion, and our way of life.

Chapter 1:

Defining Love as a Holistic Path

What is love as a religion?

Love is a holistic belief system that transcends traditional religious boundaries and emotional experiences, becoming a comprehensive framework that guides individual actions, relationships, and societal structures. Unlike conventional religions, which often focus on structured rituals and doctrines, love centers on universal principles such as compassion, empathy, altruism, and interconnectedness. This approach views love as a guiding ethos that informs ethical behaviors, spiritual connections, and practical daily actions, unifying diverse communities and fostering collective well-being.

Beyond Feelings: Love as Mindset, Belief, and Action

While emotions such as affection and passion are commonly associated with love, viewing love holistically significantly expands its scope. Love is not merely felt; it is actively practiced. It involves cultivating a mindset of kindness, empathy, and compassion that influences every interaction and decision. This holistic perspective emphasizes action—acts of kindness, intentional self-care, and socially responsible behaviors—as the practical manifestations of love.

Love is a mindset that consciously fosters positive thoughts and attitudes toward oneself and others. It encourages a deep, intrinsic commitment to acting from a place of genuine care and concern. As a guiding principle, love becomes an overarching belief that shapes personal values and ethics, guiding individuals toward choices that reflect compassion and altruism.

Love manifests concretely in daily actions such as offering help without expectation, practicing forgiveness, advocating for justice, and promoting community well-being.

The Universality of Love Across Spiritual Traditions

One of the most compelling aspects of love as a universal principle is its resonance across diverse spiritual traditions. From the compassionate teachings of Buddhism to the selfless agape of Christianity and the devotional practices of Hinduism and Sufism, love is a common thread connecting disparate beliefs and practices. This universality suggests that, despite doctrinal differences, spiritual paths converge significantly around love as a foundational principle.

For example, Buddhism emphasizes karuṇā (compassion) and mettā (loving kindness), advocating for universal benevolence. Christianity's agape encapsulates selfless, unconditional love extended universally. Hinduism's Bhakti yoga emphasizes devotional love for the divine and fosters respect for all life forms. Similarly, Sufi mysticism views divine love as the essence of existence, promoting unity and spiritual fulfillment. These convergences demonstrate how love serves as a powerful unifying force, fostering interfaith dialogue, mutual respect, and collective harmony.

Reflection: Embracing Love Beyond Emotion

Embracing "Love Beyond Emotion" challenges us to view love not as a fleeting state but as an enduring commitment that profoundly influences our ethical behavior, interpersonal connections, and societal contributions. This perspective encourages individuals to move beyond momentary feelings toward a sustained and intentional practice of love, shaping a life characterized by meaningful connections, deep empathy, and lasting positive impact.

By adopting love as a deliberate, holistic practice, we equip ourselves with resilience to overcome contemporary challenges such as isolation, digital disconnection, and social polarization. It empowers us to approach conflicts with radical compassion, heal emotional wounds with intentional kindness, and contribute actively to social progress. Ultimately, "love beyond emotion" is a call to action, inviting each person to cultivate a more compassionate, connected, and equitable world.

Chapter 2:

The Mental Dimension of Love

The Power of Loving Thoughts

Our thoughts have profound power. They shape our reality and influence how we interact with the world. Love begins in the mind as a conscious, intentional practice rather than merely an emotional reaction. When we consistently choose loving thoughts, we create a foundation for emotional resilience, psychological well-being, and meaningful connections.

Cultivating Kindness, Empathy, and Compassion

Kindness, empathy, and compassion are cornerstones of a love-centered mindset. Cultivating these qualities involves actively practicing understanding and sensitivity toward ourselves and others. Kindness begins within, as self-compassion and acceptance naturally extend outward. Empathy allows us to connect deeply with others' experiences, and compassion motivates us to act positively in the face of suffering. Regularly practicing these virtues transforms our internal dialogue and interactions with others, fostering healthier relationships and stronger communities.

Overcoming Mental Barriers to Love

Despite our best intentions, mental barriers often hinder our ability to fully embrace love. Common obstacles include self-doubt, fear of vulnerability, resentment, and ingrained biases or prejudices. It is essential to recognize and address these barriers proactively to overcome them. Mindfulness and introspection are powerful tools for identifying harmful patterns and gently shifting our perspective. We can consciously replace these barriers with loving and constructive thoughts when we become aware of them.

Exercise: Daily practices to foster loving thoughts

Consistent daily practices can profoundly influence our ability to cultivate and sustain loving thoughts:

1. **Meditation**: Engage in mindfulness or loving-kindness meditation for ten to fifteen minutes daily. Focus on breathing and visualize sending love and kindness to yourself, your loved ones, strangers, and even those with whom you struggle.

2. **Affirmations**: Write down affirmations that resonate with you, such as "I am deserving of love and kindness," "I extend compassion to everyone I meet," or "My heart is open to understanding and empathy." Recite these affirmations daily to reinforce a positive mindset.

3. **Visualization**: Regularly visualize yourself responding with love, patience, and kindness in challenging situations. Picture yourself embodying compassion and empathy, which will positively influence your interactions.

4. **Reflection**: Loving yourself to love others. Loving oneself is the essential first step toward genuinely loving others. Self-love involves appreciating your strengths, accepting your imperfections, and nurturing your emotional and physical well-being. Reflect on how your relationship with yourself shapes your interactions with others. Journal about instances where self-love improved your ability to empathize, forgive, and foster healthier relationships. Acknowledge the moments when your self-compassion translated into genuine kindness toward others.

By consciously nurturing the mental dimension of love, we pave the way for deeper, more authentic relationships and a more harmonious, fulfilling life. Embracing love as a mental discipline enriches our experiences, enhances emotional intelligence, and strengthens our connection to the world.

Chapter 3:

The Spiritual Dimension of Love

Love as a Path to Connection

At its core, love is the thread that connects us—not just to each other, but to something greater than ourselves.

Whether you call it God, the Spirit, the Universe, or simply "something more," love has always been a bridge between the seen and unseen.

Love is more than a feeling; it's a spiritual force, a vibration, a way of being that invites us into a deeper connection with the sacredness of life.

We often think of spirituality as something separate, something you do inside a church, temple, or on a meditation cushion. But what if the most spiritual thing you could do was to love fiercely, openly, and without conditions?

When we love, we touch a part of ourselves that is eternal.

Exploring Love in Diverse Spiritual Traditions

Across the world's spiritual paths, love consistently emerges as the heart of the journey.

- In Christianity, love is commanded as the highest virtue— to love God and one's neighbor and even enemies.

- In Buddhism, *mettā* (loving-kindness) meditation teaches compassion for all beings.
- In Hinduism, the path of *bhakti* is complete devotion to the Divine through love.
- Sufi mystics dance in ecstasy, seeing love as the ultimate union with the Beloved.

Even indigenous traditions often speak of love and respect for Mother Earth and all her creatures.

What's beautiful is that even with different rituals, languages, and stories, the core message is often the same:

Love is sacred. Love is the path. Love is the destination.

Chapter 4:

The Physical Dimension of Love

Love in Motion

Love is not just a feeling; it is an energy that seeks expression through action. If love stays locked in the mind or spirit without manifesting physically, it risks becoming an abstraction rather than a living force.

Love in motion is about embodying the sacred energy of love through daily habits, small gestures, and conscious choices that ripple outward into our relationships, communities, and the planet itself.

Physical love is the bridge between the invisible and the tangible. It's how love touches and transforms the world. When we move with love—through a smile, a touch, a kind word, or a helping hand—we breathe life into the idea that love is our religion.

Expressing Love Through Action and Habits

The power of love is multiplied when it becomes habitual. Love expands through consistent, thoughtful action as a tree grows through daily nourishment. Loving actions aren't reserved for grand occasions; they happen in the seemingly mundane details:

- Checking on a friend when you sense they're having a hard time

- Leaving a kind note for a family member
- Volunteering your time without seeking recognition
- Offering a genuine compliment to a stranger

When we make loving actions a part of our daily rhythm, we reinforce love as a way of being rather than a sporadic feeling.

Physical Expressions: Touch, Kindness, Acts of Service
Physical expressions of love are a universal language that transcends words. They create a bridge of connection across cultural, language, and belief divides.

Touch: A hug, a handshake, or a pat on the back conveys warmth, affirmation, and acceptance. Healthy, consensual physical contact nurtures bonds and promotes emotional healing.

Kindness: Even the smallest acts of kindness can carry profound weight. Paying for someone's coffee, holding a door open, or simply listening attentively to another person are tangible expressions of love.

Acts of service: Doing something meaningful for someone else without expectation of return embodies love in action. Whether cooking a meal, helping someone move, or cleaning a public space, these acts of service ripple outward, inspiring more love.

These expressions are simple, but their impact is powerful and far-reaching.

Exercise: Daily Practices to Embody Love

To integrate the physical dimension of love into your life, try the following simple daily practices:

- **Morning intention**: Each morning, set the intention: *"Today, I will embody love through at least one action."*
- **Touch with care**: Offer at least one meaningful, appropriate touch each day—a hug, a handshake, or a comforting hand on the shoulder.
- **Kindness countdown**: Aim for three small acts of kindness daily, no matter how small.
- **Service Sundays**: Dedicate a portion of each Sunday (or another day) to an act of service for others—family, community, or planet.

Consistency is key. Over time, these small daily practices will reshape how you move through the world: not just thinking love, believing love, but **being love**.

Reflection: Extending Love to the Planet and Community

Love cannot be confined to personal relationships alone. True love spills over into a passion for the world—the Earth we live on, the communities we are part of, the generations that will come after us.

Environmental Responsibility

Loving the planet means taking conscious steps to protect it. Reducing waste, conserving resources, and supporting eco-friendly initiatives are all physical manifestations of love. The Earth is our shared home, and stewardship is an act of collective affection and responsibility.

Social Engagement

Community love manifests through participation and care. Volunteering, activism, and advocating for justice are powerful ways to put love into action at a societal level. Love calls us to extend our circle of care beyond ourselves, our families, and even our immediate communities to embrace all beings.

Closing Thought for the Chapter:

"Love is not something we feel—it is something we live. In every breath, every touch, every act of kindness, love takes on a physical form—and through us, it reaches the world."

Chapter 5:

Navigating Love in the Modern World

Loving in the Age of Disconnection

Love, once a thread that wove communities and hearts tightly together, now faces new challenges. In an age where technology connects us faster than ever, it paradoxically also pulls us apart. A text message cannot replace the warmth of a smile. A "like" on a photo can never substitute for genuine understanding. We are more "connected" yet more isolated.

As we navigate this digital era, our task is not to resist technology but to reclaim the depth and sincerity of our connections. Love must evolve, becoming even more intentional and radical in its compassion.

The Impact of Technology and Social Media on Love

The digital landscape has reshaped how we express affection, meet one another, and sustain our relationships. Yet love often gets lost amidst endless scrolling, curated highlight reels, and the dopamine hits of notifications.

Technology offers us incredible tools for connection, such as video calls with loved ones across oceans, group chats that keep friendships alive, and dating apps that create new possibilities. But, when left unchecked, it can also foster comparison, superficiality, and loneliness.

To love deeply in the digital age, we must **pause and reflect**.

We must ask:

- Are we truly connecting or simply communicating?
- Are we seeking validation or offering a genuine presence?

Real love demands more than quick clicks. It asks for patience, vulnerability, and courage to sit in silence with someone and truly listen.

Building Meaningful Connections in a Digital Age

So, how do we build meaningful bonds amidst the noise?

- **Slow down**: Deep connections are nurtured over time. Allow conversations to unfold naturally without rushing toward an outcome.
- **Be present**: When you are with someone—physically or virtually—be fully there. Put away distractions. Make eye contact. Listen to understand, not to respond.
- **Lead with authenticity**: Let people see the real you—the unfiltered, imperfect, beautiful human behind the screen.
- **Practice digital mindfulness**: Set intentional boundaries around your tech use. Prioritize in-person interactions whenever possible.

Love in a digital world requires intentionality. It's about choosing depth over convenience. It's about being fully human in a system that often reduces us to avatars.

Radical Compassion

Radical compassion is the revolutionary act of choosing love when fear, anger, or indifference would be the easier option.

It's easy to love those who agree with us, who look like us, who make us feel good. Genuine radical compassion is loving beyond one's comfort zone, embracing the difficult, the different, and even the "enemy."

This doesn't mean tolerating abuse or allowing ourselves to be harmed. It means recognizing humanity in all beings, even when it's hard to see.

Radical compassion asks:
- Can I stay open-hearted even when I'm hurt?
- Can I choose understanding over judgment?
- Can I extend grace to those who themselves may be deeply wounded?

When we answer yes, even imperfectly, even hesitantly, we embody love in its highest form.

Love as a Response to Conflict and Division

Our world is increasingly polarized. Political debates, cultural differences, and personal misunderstandings tear at the fabric of our communities.

But conflict need not be the end of love. It can be the beginning.

When we respond to division with love:
- We listen to learn, not to win.
- We seek common ground, not battlefields.
- We remember that every argument, every harsh word, is an opportunity to sow seeds of understanding instead of bitterness.

Love as a response to conflict is not a weakness but a courageous strength. It is choosing creation over destruction, healing over harm.

Practicing Forgiveness and Empathy

Forgiveness is not about condoning wrongs or erasing pain. It's about setting ourselves free from the heavy chains of resentment. It is a gift we give ourselves, even more than the person who hurt us.

Empathy—the ability to step into another's shoes—is forgiveness's twin flame. When we practice empathy, we soften the walls around our hearts. We recognize that everyone is carrying burdens we cannot see.

To practice forgiveness and empathy:
- Acknowledge your hurt without judgment.
- Choose to see the woundedness behind others' actions.
- Release the need for revenge or a sense of "rightness" and embrace peace instead.

Forgiveness and empathy do not alter the past, but they can transform the future.

Reflection: Choosing Compassion over Division
Take a quiet moment. Reflect on a relationship, a situation, or even a public issue that has stirred anger or division in your heart.

Ask yourself:
- Where can I bring more understanding?
- How can I show compassion without compromising my truth?
- What small act of love could I offer today to bridge the gap?

Whenever we choose compassion over division, we help heal our world and the larger world we share.

Love is not a passive feeling. It is an active choice. It is the way forward.

Chapter 6:

The Healing Power of Love

Healing Through Love

Love is not only an emotional experience but a profound force of healing. It can mend broken hearts, ease wounded minds, and nurture resilience. When we embrace love for ourselves, others, and life itself, we invite emotional, mental, and even physical healing into our lives. Love soothes the fractures created by pain and trauma, reawakening our innate wholeness.

Love reminds us that healing is not about forgetting the pain but transforming it. It's about recognizing and meeting our wounds with compassion rather than judgment. When we approach ourselves and others with genuine love, we create the conditions necessary for true healing to take root.

Love's Role in Emotional and Mental Health

Numerous studies and traditions support the notion that love enhances mental and emotional well-being. Self-love, encompassing setting healthy boundaries, practicing forgiveness, and cultivating positive self-talk, is essential in developing emotional resilience. Similarly, giving and receiving love from others contributes to reduced anxiety, depression, and feelings of isolation.

When we practice love consistently, it:
- reduces stress hormones like cortisol.

- enhances the release of "feel-good" chemicals, such as oxytocin and dopamine.
- improves emotional regulation and strengthens emotional resilience.
- encourages a deep sense of connection, meaning, and purpose.

Love becomes a revolutionary healing practice in a world that often promotes achievement over connection, restoring balance, meaning, and hope.

Overcoming Trauma, Anxiety, and Depression

Trauma fractures our sense of safety and self-worth. Anxiety amplifies fear and uncertainty. Depression convinces us we are alone in our suffering. When intentionally cultivated, love serves as a balm for all these wounds.

Healing through love involves:

- **Self-compassion:** Meeting your pain with kindness rather than criticism.
- **Forgiveness:** Letting go of resentment toward yourself and others to lighten your emotional burden.
- **Connection:** Building authentic relationships where you feel seen, heard, and valued.
- **Meaning-making:** Reframing painful experiences as opportunities for growth and more profound empathy.

It's not about "fixing" yourself. It's about *loving* yourself into wholeness again and again.

Exercise: Strengthening Your "Love Muscles"
Like physical muscles, your capacity for love strengthens through consistent, intentional practice. Here are daily "love muscle" exercises:

1. Self-Affection Practice:
Every morning, look into a mirror and say something kind and affirming to yourself. Speak to yourself as if you were someone you deeply love.

2. Gratitude List:
Before bed, write down three things you love about your day or yourself. Gratitude cultivates a loving perspective.

3. Loving-Kindness Meditation (Metta):
Spend five minutes sending silent well-wishes to yourself, loved ones, strangers, and even those with whom you have complicated relationships.

4. Acts of Kindness:
Do one unexpected act of kindness each day, even something small. Notice how it feels to give love freely.

5. Emotional Check-Ins:

Ask yourself daily: "What do I need to feel loved and supported?" Honor the answer without judgment.

Practical Challenges to Grow Your Capacity for Love

Growing in love sometimes requires stretching beyond our comfort zones. Here are some challenges to spark growth:

- *Forgive someone who hurt you (even silently).*
- *Have an honest conversation about your feelings.*
- *Offer help without expectation of reciprocity.*
- *Compliment a stranger.*
- *Set a loving boundary without guilt.*
- *Spend a day without negative self-talk.*
- *Write a letter or email of thanks to someone who impacted your life.*

These challenges are not about perfection. They're about practicing the vulnerability and courage that love demands.

Reflection: Love as a Healer

What would change if you treated yourself as someone worthy of deep love and compassion every single day?
How might your wounds transform if you approached them as invitations to greater love, not shame?

Healing through love is not a one-time act but a lifelong commitment.

Each moment you choose love for yourself and others, you choose to heal.

Chapter 7:

Love as a Collective Force

Global Love: Creating a Ripple Effect

Love does not end with personal transformation; it expands outward, rippling across communities and eventually influencing the wider world. Every act of kindness, every moment of compassion, and every decision guided by love collectively contribute to a momentum toward a more harmonious society. This chapter explores how individual acts of love, when multiplied, become a force powerful enough to shift cultures, drive justice, and build a better future for all.

How Individual Acts of Love Inspire Societal Change

One person's act of love might seem small, but its impact often extends far beyond the moment it occurs. A smile can soften anger. A random act of generosity can inspire another. Courageous forgiveness can dismantle walls of resentment that separate families, neighborhoods, and even nations.

Movements for social change often begin with individuals choosing love over fear or indifference. From grassroots humanitarian efforts to widespread peace campaigns, history is full of examples of how personal convictions rooted in love have sparked transformations at national and global levels.

- **Historical example:** Rosa Parks' refusal to give up her seat wasn't an act of civil disobedience but a love for human dignity.

- **Everyday ripple effects:** A teacher encouraging empathy among students, planting seeds that will bloom into more compassionate communities.

The important truth is this: when you practice love consistently, you can help shape the world's collective emotional and moral atmosphere.

Movements and Stories of Collective Love in Action
Throughout history, collective love has manifested in movements and communities that refuse to accept injustice, inequality, or hatred.

- **The Civil Rights Movement** in the United States was fueled by love for freedom and human dignity.
- **Mahatma Gandhi's nonviolent resistance** in India demonstrated satyagraha—truth-force or love-force—opposing injustice without resorting to violence or hatred.
- **Modern environmental movements** are often driven by deep love for the planet and future generations.

Even smaller, lesser-known examples show the profound potential of collective love:

- Community gardens that feed struggling families
- Local volunteers organize refugee resettlement programs

- Acts of solidarity after natural disasters, where strangers open their homes and hearts

Love moves people toward *action*, often without asking for anything in return. And when enough individuals move together, guided by love, things can change.

Reflection: Love as Social Activism

What would it look like to treat activism not merely as resistance but as an expression of radical love?

Social activism rooted in anger alone may burn out or divide, but activism fueled by love endures and builds bridges. Loving activism asks:

- *How can I advocate for justice while still honoring the dignity of every human involved, even those with whom I disagree?*
- *How can I show compassion to those who have caused harm without excusing their actions?*

Love doesn't mean passivity. It means fighting for what's right *because* you care about others' well-being, freedom, and dignity as deeply as your own. It's an activism that seeks healing, not revenge.

Reflection questions:

- Where in your community do you see love already working toward justice?
- How can your everyday actions be more intentionally tied to collective healing and change?

Engaging in Compassionate Action for Justice and Equity

Engaging in collective love begins with simple choices:

- Listen deeply to those whose experiences are different from your own.
- Support initiatives that promote equality, fairness, and compassion.
- Volunteer your time and talents to uplift the vulnerable.
- Advocate for policies that center on human dignity and environmental stewardship.
- Choose empathy even when it's uncomfortable.

You don't have to join a global movement to create change. Love-inspired action starts with how you show up daily—in your conversations, spending choices, and willingness to stand up when it matters.

In truth, every act of love—no matter how small—is an act of activism.

Chapter 8:

Bringing it All Together – A Love Manifesto

Living a Love-Centered Life

Throughout this journey, we've explored love beyond fleeting emotions. We've witnessed how love can permeate the mind, spirit, and body, creating a more intentional, connected, and whole life. Living a love-centered life is not about achieving perfection; it is about embracing an evolving practice in which love serves as the compass guiding your thoughts, actions, and connections.

A love-centered life means choosing kindness when anger is easier, understanding when judgment feels more natural, and choosing presence when distraction beckons. It's about embodying love daily in small, consistent ways until it becomes who you are, not just something you do.

Love as an Ongoing, Evolving Journey

Love is not a destination. It's a living, breathing practice that evolves with you. Some days, love feels effortless. Other days, it feels like a mountain you're unsure you can climb. Both are part of the journey.

To live a love-centered life means accepting that imperfection is part of growth. Mistakes are not signs of failure but invitations to deepen one's practice of compassion, for oneself and others. **Love is a lifelong teacher**, inviting you to grow in wisdom, resilience, humility, and grace.

Exercise: Creating Your Personal Love Creed

Your love creed is your personal manifesto, a living document that captures your intention to embody love fully and authentically.

Steps to Create Your Personal Love Creed:

1. **Reflect**: What does love mean to you beyond emotion? What values arise when you live through love?

2. **Write your core principles**: List five to ten principles or affirmations that you want to guide your life (example: "I choose compassion over judgment" or "I will speak with kindness even when it is difficult").

3. **Create a daily reminder**: Post your love creed somewhere visible—on your mirror, desk, or phone wallpaper—so you can read it every day.

4. **Evolve it**: Revisit and refine your creed every six to twelve months. As you grow, so will your understanding and embodiment of love.

Developing Guiding Principles for a Life of Holistic Love

Here are a few universal principles to inspire your love creed:

- **Kindness before reaction**: Respond with compassion before reacting with ego.
- **Presence over distraction**: Practice being fully present with yourself and others.
- **Empathy over assumption**: Seek to understand rather than assume.
- **Service over selfishness**: Give your love in service to the greater good.
- **Gratitude over entitlement**: Appreciate the beauty of existence, even in its imperfections.

These guiding lights help you weave love into the fabric of your daily life—in your thoughts, relationships, and service to the world.

Reflection and Forward Movement

This book is not the end of the journey—it's just the beginning.

Reflection Questions:

- How has your understanding of love evolved during this journey?
- What habits or practices have you developed that strengthen your capacity to love?
- In what areas of your life would you like to deepen your practice of holistic love?

Forward Movement:

- **Set intentions**: What small, meaningful actions can you take this week to embody your love creed?
- **Create community**: Share your love journey with others. Love grows when it is shared.
- **Stay open**: Allow love to evolve you. Stay open to growth, even when it's uncomfortable.

Setting Intentions for Continued Growth and Connection

- **Daily love practices**: Meditate, journal, or practice mindfulness to nurture love.
- **Weekly reflections**: Once a week, reflect on how you practiced love and where you can grow.
- **Community engagement**: Practice collective love by volunteering, supporting community initiatives, and advocating for justice and compassion.
- **Continual learning**: Read, listen, and engage with ideas that challenge you to expand your understanding and expression of love.

Remember:

You are a ripple in the ocean of humanity.
When you live from love, you send out waves that reach farther than you can imagine.

Love is not a religion you practice once a week.

It is a revolution in which you live every day.

Conclusion

A Vision for the Future: Embracing a World Transformed by Love

As we stand at the threshold of an evolving world, the invitation before us is profound: to choose love as the guiding force that shapes our future. Throughout this journey, we have explored love not simply as an emotion but as a holistic way of life—a philosophy, a spiritual path, and a practical framework for living fully in mind, body, and spirit.

Envision a future where individuals awaken each day with love as their primary intention, where compassion naturally flows into our conversations, actions, and communities, and where differences are not reasons for division but opportunities for deeper understanding and connection. In such a world, love is not an occasional act or a reserved feeling—it is the very fabric of society.

This vision asks us to be active creators, not passive dreamers. Love must be embodied daily—in our thoughts, choices, interactions, and commitments to justice, healing, and unity. It means extending compassion when judgment feels easier, offering kindness when apathy tempts us, and standing for others even when it requires courage.

Imagine the collective power unleashed when individuals around the world commit to living love as a religion—not bound by dogma but illuminated by universal principles of care, respect, and connection. Education systems could nurture empathy alongside knowledge. Governments could craft policies rooted in dignity and human flourishing. Communities could become ecosystems of belonging, resilience, and joy.

Of course, this future is not without its challenges. Skepticism, resistance, and the inertia of old systems will persist. Yet, love—persistent, patient, and profound—has always been humanity's greatest agent of transformation.

As history has shown, even small acts of love can ripple outward to inspire extraordinary change.

Today, we are called to be the seeds of that transformation.

The choice is ours to make, moment by moment, breath by breath.

Let us move forward with open hearts, bold spirits, and a deep commitment to living love completely—for ourselves, one another, and the generations to come.

Love is not merely the way. Love is the future. And together, we are its creators.

Additional Tools and Resources

This section provides tools and resources to support your success, wealth, and overall well-being, encouraging a life of genuine love.

MindSafe©

Creating a safe and nurturing environment for your mental well-being.

1. **Firewall your mind**: Think of your mind as a firewall that protects your mental well-being. Establish firm mental boundaries to filter incoming information. Just as a firewall blocks unauthorized access, set clear boundaries regarding the information you allow into your mind. This involves being selective about the sources and opinions you expose yourself to.

2. **Develop an "antiviral" mindset**: Develop a mindset that acts as an antivirus program, scanning and filtering incoming information. Train yourself to be discerning, critical, and skeptical of ideas or beliefs that may harm your mental well-being. This proactive approach helps you identify and neutralize potential threats before they impact your mindset.

3. **Regularly update your mental software**: Just as computer security systems require regular updates, make it a habit to update your mental software through learning and personal growth. Stay open to new ideas, knowledge, and perspectives, and consciously integrate them into your belief system. This ongoing development helps you adapt and strengthen your mental defenses.

4. **Create a "quarantine" for negativity**: Like a computer system quarantines suspicious files, establish a mental quarantine for negative thoughts, emotions, and opinions. When you encounter harmful or toxic information, consciously acknowledge its presence but avoid allowing it to permeate your mental space. Focus on positive and constructive thoughts instead.

5. **Encrypt your core beliefs**: Encryption protects sensitive data, making it unreadable to unauthorized users. Encrypt your core beliefs by deepening your understanding and reinforcing them with solid reasoning and evidence. This way, external influences are less likely to sway you from your core values and principles.

6. **Practice regular mental "system scans:"** Set aside time for introspection and self-reflection, similar to running system scans on a computer. Regularly evaluate your thoughts, emotions, and beliefs to ensure they align with your values. Determine whether they align with your core values and overall well-being. Identify any potential vulnerabilities or areas where external influences may negatively impact you.

7. **Backup and restore your mental well-being**: Just as you create backups of important data, prioritize self-care and well-being practices as a form of mental backup. Engage in activities

that recharge you, bring you joy, and restore your mental balance. This ensures you have a reservoir of positivity and resilience to draw upon when facing external influences.

8. **Employ a solid authentication system (self-validation):** Protect your mental well-being using a reliable authentication system of self-confidence and self-assuredness. Trust in your judgment and intuition. Develop a strong sense of self-resistance to external pressures and opinions. This helps you stay grounded and true to yourself.

Remember that computer and data security systems are helpful metaphors for protecting your mental health. Tailor these concepts to suit your journey in maintaining your well-being. Continuously revisit and modify your strategies as you encounter various circumstances and obstacles.

Kevin J. Houston

The Stoic Lifestyle Playbook

Core Philosophical Principles

1. Dichotomy of Control

• Focus on what you can control: your thoughts, choices, and actions.

• Let go of external events, they're not up to you.

2. Live According to Nature

• Align with reason and virtue.

• Act honestly, justly, courageously, and with self-discipline.

3. Amor Fati - Love Your Fate

• Embrace every experience as valuable.

• Don't resist reality, adapt and grow.

4. Memento Mori - Remember You Will Die

• Reflect on mortality to focus on what matters.

• Use your time wisely.

5. Sympatheia - Universal Brotherhood

• See all people as part of a whole.

• Practice compassion, patience, and justice.

Daily Stoic Practices

1. **Morning**:

• **Pre-meditation:** Reflect on likely challenges and how to respond with virtue.

• **Set intentions:** Ask, "How can I act with wisdom, justice, courage, and temperance today?"

• **Journaling prompts:** What is in my control today? What virtue will I practice?

2. **During the Day**:

• **Practice the pause**: Before reacting, ask if it's under your control.

• **Voluntary discomfort:** Use challenges to build resilience.

• **Micro reflections:** Check in. Are you being guided by virtue?

3. **Evening**:

• **Review the day:** What went well? Where can you improve?

• **Gratitude:** Appreciate without attachment.

4. **Weekly & Monthly Practices**

• **Negative visualization:** Imagine a loss to train appreciation and readiness in your mind.

• **Read stoic texts:** Meditations (Aurelius), letters (Seneca), discourses (Epictetus).

• **Service to others:** Be kind without recognition.

• Silence Practice: Reflect without digital distractions.

5. Long-Term Habits

• **Minimalism:** Simplify your life.

• **Discipline:** Train your will.

• **Accountability:** Use a journal or partner to hold yourself accountable.

• **Study philosophy:** Deepen your understanding.

• **Accept fate, act intentionally:** Combine acceptance with purpose.

6. Stoic Affirmations

•" I control how I respond."

•" Obstacles are opportunities in disguise."

• "What matters is how I live, not what I suffer."

•" I need little to be happy."

•" Virtue is enough."

The 40-Day Practice of Love

A daily immersion in awareness, compassion, and conscious living.

Purpose:

A daily pilgrimage inward and outward—forty small steps to retrain the heart, the mind, and the body to move in rhythm with love.

Each week carries a theme that deepens the practice.

Introduction

Love grows through repetition. Not grand gestures, but the quiet, daily kind. This forty-day practice is a training ground for the heart—forty invitations to notice, soften, and choose love in motion. Move through them one day at a time, one breath at a time.

Week 1 – Awakening to Love

Theme: Awareness and gratitude.
Love begins with seeing—seeing what's already good, what's already whole.

- **Practice:** Each morning, name one quality of love you wish to embody today: patience, presence, kindness.
- **Journal:** Five moments that stirred gratitude, however small.
- **Mindfulness:** When irritation arises, pause. Ask, "How would love see this?"
- **Reflection:** "If I made love my first response, how would my day change?"

Week 2 – Loving the Self

Theme: Self-compassion and restoration.
Before love can flow outward, it must find safe ground within you.

- **Practice:** List three things you forgive yourself for.
- **Body care:** Rest or nourish yourself without apology.

- **Mantra:** "I am worthy of gentle care."
- **Reflection:** Notice how self-kindness softens your view of others.

Week 3 – Love in a Relationship

Theme: Connection and empathy.
Love thrives in attention.

- **Practice:** Give one person your undivided focus—no devices, no multitasking.
- **Act:** Offer gratitude to someone you've overlooked.
- **Repair:** Apologize where needed; listen without defense.
- **Reflection:** "When I listen deeply, what changes in me?"

Week 4 – Love in Action

Theme: Service and presence.
Love is a verb with a heartbeat.

- **Practice:** Do one act of kindness anonymously.
- **Stewardship:** Pick up litter, water a neglected plant, check on a neighbor.
- **Slow down:** Replace haste with patience once today.
- **Reflection:** "How can my hands become instruments of love?"

Week 5 – Expanding Love

Theme: Compassion beyond comfort.
True love stretches the circle wider.

- **Practice:** Learn about a perspective unlike your own.
- **Meditate:** Send compassion to someone who tests your patience.
- **Speak:** Use your voice kindly against injustice.
- **Reflection:** "Where is love inviting me to grow larger than my fear?"

Week 6 – Embodying Love

Theme: Integration and celebration.
The work now is to live what you've learned.

- **Revisit:** Read your early journal pages—what shifted?
- **Move:** Walk, dance, or stretch as a thank you to your body.
- **Create:** Write your *Love Creed*—a simple paragraph beginning with "I choose…"
- **Ritual:** Light a candle, speak your intention aloud, and offer thanks.
- **Closing reflection:** "Love is not something I feel—it's what I've become willing to practice."

The 7 Paths of Living Love

A lifelong map for keeping love at the center

1. The Path of Awareness

To love is to see clearly. Cultivate mindfulness; pause long enough to notice beauty, breathe, and your needs. Gratitude is awareness in motion.

Practice prompt: Begin and end each day by naming three blessings you almost missed.

2. The Path of Compassion

Compassion is empathy that has learned to walk. It listens, then acts.

Reflection question: Where can I turn understanding into tangible help today?

3. The Path of Truth

Love cannot live in pretense. Speak gently, but do not hide. Integrity is love's backbone.

Practice prompt: Say what is true for you today without armor or performance.

4. The Path of Forgiveness

Forgiveness releases the past so love can breathe again.

Reflection question: Who or what still occupies space in my heart rent-free? Am I ready to let go?

5. The Path of Service

Service is how love shows its hands. Every gift—skill, word, resource—is a chance to mend something.

Practice prompt: Offer one act of service this week with no expectation of anything in return.

6. The Path of Unity

We are threads in one fabric. Unity asks us to honor difference while remembering our shared pulse.

Reflection question: How can I collaborate instead of compete?

7. The Path of Joy

Joy is love realized—the laughter, the dance, the awe. It reminds us that love's work is not always heavy.

Practice prompt: Do one thing today purely for delight.

Applied Love:

Living principles in everyday life

1. Love at Work

Theme: Turning ambition into service.
Most of us spend more waking hours at work than anywhere else, yet rarely see it as sacred ground. Love at work isn't about soft smiles or avoiding accountability—it's about remembering that the people around you are not roles but lives in progress. Love turns the grind into purpose.

Practices
- **Begin with intention:** Before opening an email, ask, *"Who might benefit from what I do today?"* It shifts you from self-protection to contribution.
- **Communicate with clarity:** Vague feedback wounds more than blunt honesty ever could. Speak truth with tone, not temper.
- **Honor limits:** Overworking in the name of dedication breeds resentment. Rest keeps your compassion usable.
- **Recognize effort:** Simple words like "I see what you did there" can foster a sense of belonging more than formal praise.

Reflection:
Where in my work have I mistaken pressure for purpose? What would leadership look like if it began with empathy instead of authority?

2. Love in Conflict

Theme: Staying human when tension rises.
Conflict is inevitable wherever people care. Love doesn't erase disagreement—it changes the posture you bring to it. When tempers flare, the goal isn't to win but to understand.

Practices
- **Pause before reacting:** Breathe, then restate what you heard. Most battles shrink under accurate translation.
- **Stay curious:** Ask, "What matters most to you right now?" rather than defending your view.

- **Name the emotion, not the enemy:** "I feel dismissed" invites dialogue; "You never listen" invites war.
- **Repair quickly:** After arguments, return—even with a small gesture. It conveys the idea that the relationship matters more than the issue.

Reflection:

Can I stay rooted in respect even when I'm right? Where does love invite me to listen longer than is comfortable?

3. Love and Technology

Theme: Presence in the digital blur.
We live half-inside glass rectangles that reflect more of ourselves than we realize. Love and technology can coexist—but only if we treat our attention like a finite resource, not free currency.

Practices

- **Curate your inputs:** Follow accounts that expand empathy, not anxiety. Your feed becomes your inner voice.
- **Practice "digital eye contact:"** When messaging, picture the person's humanity—tone softens naturally.
- **Set sacred hours:** Mornings or meals without screens remind the body that presence still exists in the offline world.
- **Respond, don't react:** Type slower. Re-read before sending. Love edits.

Reflection:

Does my digital footprint leave a lasting impression or residue? How can I make my online life reflect my real values?

4. Love and Leadership

Theme: Influence with humility.
Leadership magnifies whatever lives inside you. Fear breeds control; love breeds trust. A leader grounded in love holds authority lightly and people firmly.

Practices

- **Listen before directing:** Begin meetings with one genuine question. Curiosity disarms hierarchy.
- **Model vulnerability:** Admit when you don't know; it gives others permission to be honest.
- **Empower over impress:** Share credit publicly, mentor privately, and step aside to allow others to shine.
- **Hold boundaries with grace:** Compassion doesn't mean chaos; clarity is kindness in disguise.

Reflection:
Do those I lead feel safer or smaller around me? Am I building followers or cultivating leaders?

5. Love in Loss

Theme: Holding grief without hardening.
Loss cracks us open to what remains eternal. Grief is not the absence of love—it's love without a place to land. Allowing pain to move through you keeps tenderness alive.

Practices

- **Honor the ache:** Sit with the feeling without rushing to "get over it." Healing starts when sorrow is witnessed, not silenced.
- **Create a ritual:** Light a candle, keep a photo, write a letter. Repetition turns remembrance into reverence.
- **Stay connected:** Reach for others; grief isolates by instinct. Presence from another heart regulates your own.
- **Turn loss into legacy:** Channel love into acts that continue what or who you lost—volunteering, storytelling, mentoring.

Reflection:
How has grief deepened my compassion for others' pain? What part of love still lives on quietly inside the ache?

6. Love and the Planet

Theme: Extending care beyond the human circle.
The Earth teaches reciprocity: nothing truly belongs to us, yet everything depends on our choices. Love for the planet begins with awe, not guilt.

Practices
- **Notice the ordinary sacred:** The smell of rain, the hum of bees—attention itself is an act of reverence.
- **Tread lightly:** Reduce waste, reuse more, and repair rather than replace. Small habits multiplied by millions shift futures.
- **Support stewardship:** Buy from those who protect, not exploit. Vote with your wallet and your voice.
- **Educate and include:** Bring children, friends, or community into simple earth-honoring rituals, planting, cleaning, and observing.

Reflection:
If the planet is an extension of myself, how do I show self-love through how I live on it?

7. Love and Community

Theme: Building circles of care.
We heal fastest in connection. Community is the body through which love circulates—a living network of witness, support, and accountability.

Practices
- **Start small:** Learn names, share food, show up consistently. Community grows through repetition, not events.
- **Offer belonging, not agreement:** Create spaces where difference isn't danger. Listening is the most radical inclusion.
- **Exchange generosity:** Let others help you, too; reciprocity keeps dignity intact.

- **Anchor in shared purpose:** Whether through service, art, or conversation, build something that outlives convenience.

Reflection:
What gifts do I bring to my community's table? How can I make others feel seen just by being around me?

Love is not an escape from the world's mess; it's a way of walking through it without losing warmth. These applied practices are invitations, not perfection checklists.

Wherever you work, argue, scroll, lead, grieve, plant, or gather, love can take up residence and quietly change the atmosphere.

The Discipline of Gentleness

Gentleness is not weakness. It is a quiet strength—the art of meeting the world without sharpening our edges.

When love matures, it becomes gentle. It learns that transformation does not always come through force, but through steady presence and a willingness to understand.

To be gentle is to hold space for what is fragile—within others and within ourselves. It is choosing to respond instead of react, to breathe before speaking, to see another person not as an obstacle but as someone carrying their own unseen weight.

Gentleness enables us to navigate conflict without compromising compassion and to convey truth without cruelty.

Love requires this discipline. Gentleness is not always our first instinct when we are hurt, hurried, or afraid. It must be practiced like any spiritual muscle. It begins with how we treat ourselves: softening the voice that criticizes,
easing the pressure to perform, allowing rest to be sacred.

From there, gentleness spills outward—into our words, our homes, our work.

When gentleness meets strength, love becomes enduring. It can correct without shaming, lead without dominating, and hold boundaries without closing off the heart.

Gentle people are not passive; they are clear, anchored, and able to bend without breaking.

In a culture that prizes urgency and noise, gentleness feels radical. It slows us down long enough to notice the sacred in the ordinary—the tone of our speech, the touch of a hand, the way we listen. Each moment becomes an altar for kindness.

Practicing gentleness is an act of faith: faith that loves does not need to overpower to be effective, faith that is patient can heal more deeply than punishment, tender faith, consistently lived, reshapes even the most challenging environments.

Gentleness is love wearing wisdom. It is the quiet courage to meet life with open hands, again and again—trusting that what we offer in softness will ripple farther than anything we could force into place.

Acknowledgements

I would like to express my sincere gratitude to the many individuals who supported and inspired me throughout my life and in the writing of this book.

First, I would like to give the most heartfelt thanks to my wife, Kerensa, for the encouragement, motivation and strength to complete this book and continue to be the man I am. The love she has shown me in her daily life was an inspiration for this book. She is my queen, my life partner, and the person I am glad to have by my side on this journey of love.

I am also profoundly grateful to my mom, Daisy, for helping me to become the man that I am. She has been there for me through all of my ups and downs in life from the beginning until now.

I would like to give special thanks to my brothers and sisters for their unwavering encouragement and support throughout my life in everything I have set out to do and achieve.

I would like to thank all my children for being the encouragement and push that has motivated me to continue my mission in life as a teacher, encourager, and motivator.

Finally, I would like to extend a sincere thank you and gratitude to all of my family and friends—past and present, near and far. I have learned from and shared much with many of you throughout my life's journey. You have all been a source of knowledge, education, and inspiration to me during the times we have shared.

One final personal note, I would like to give a special thanks to the Marley (Bob Marley) family for the message of love in the music they share with the world.

www.ingramcontent.com/pod-product-compliance
Lightning Source LLC
LaVergne TN
LVHW021538080426
835509LV00019B/2718